To Gre

Thanks for your love

and all the many

times you help me.

Much love,

Aunt Jo

Cover design and illustrations by Cheryl Benner
Design by Dawn J. Ranck

SOUPS: THE BEST OF FAVORITE RECIPES FROM QUILTERS

International Standard Book Number: 1-56148-112-2
Library of Congress Catalog Card Number: 94-14901

Library of Congress Cataloging-in-Publication Data

Soups / [compiled by] Louise Stoltzfus.
p. cm. — (The Best of Favorite recipes from quilters)
Includes index.
ISBN 1-56148-112-2 : $7.95
1. Soups. I. Stoltzfus, Louise, 1952- . II> Series.
TX757.S63433 1994
641.8'13—dc20

94-14901
CIP

Introduction

Amid the rush and haste of life, many people seek rest and quiet in community life. Quilters find community in common goals and activities. They talk of needles and thread, fabric and stitches, and bedcovers and pieces of art. They gather in homes, fabric shops, and convention centers to share their ideas and projects.

Many quilters are also homemakers. Some treat both cooking and quilting as high art forms. Others work hard to prepare varied and healthful meals for their busy families and quilt when they have free time.

From Oyster Stew to Baked Onion Soup to Hearty French Market Bean Soup, these Soup recipes are both practical and delicious. Those who love to quilt and those who love to cook will share in the special vibrancy of this small collection.

Hearty French Market Bean Soup

Mitzi McGlynchey, Downingtown, PA

1 lb. assorted beans
2 quarts water
1 quart chicken stock
1 Tbsp. salt
1 ham hock
2 bay leaves
½ tsp. dried thyme
28-oz. can tomatoes, chopped
2 cups chopped onion
2 cups chopped celery
1 clove garlic, mashed
8 ozs. smoked sausage, sliced
8 ozs. chicken breast, diced

1. Wash and soak beans at least 2 hours, preferably overnight.
2. In a large soup kettle combine beans, water, stock, salt, ham hock, bay leaves and thyme. Cover and simmer for 2½-3 hours.
3. Add tomatoes, onion and celery. Cover and simmer 1½ hours.
4. Add garlic, sausage and chicken. Cover and simmer 40 minutes. Serve.

Makes 10-12 servings

Black Bean Soup

Kelly Wagoner, Albuquerque, NM

3 cups dry black beans
6-8 cups water
1 Tbsp. cooking oil
3 Tbsp. honey
4 carrots, chopped
1 large onion, chopped
3 stalks celery, chopped
1 green bell pepper, chopped
Salt and pepper (optional)
1 whole orange

1. Soak washed beans 2-3 hours or overnight. Cook beans in water, oil and honey until tender. (To speed process, precook beans for 5 minutes in pressure cooker.) Put through blender.
2. Return blended beans to soup pot. Add vegetables and orange which has been cut in half. Simmer 45 minutes to 1 hour or until vegetables are tender. Gently squeeze out orange halves into soup and discard shells. Serve.

Note: *This wonderful vegetarian's soup is delightful served with homemade whole wheat bread. Better the second day.*

Makes 3 quarts soup

Wild Rice Soup

Lee Ann Hazlett, Freeport, IL

½ lb. bacon
1 onion, diced
½ cup chopped celery
3 Tbsp. butter or *margarine*
3 Tbsp. flour
½ tsp. thyme
½ tsp. paprika
1 Tbsp. Worcestershire sauce
10¾-oz. can chicken broth
2 cups milk
1 cup cooked wild rice

1. Fry, drain and crumble bacon. Set aside.
2. Sauté onion and celery in butter. Stir in flour, thyme and paprika and heat until bubbly. Add Worcestershire sauce, chicken broth and milk and heat, stirring until thickened.
3. Fold in wild rice and bacon and serve.

Makes 6 servings

Elegant Wild Rice Soup

Jean Swift, Comfrey, MN

2 Tbsp. butter
1 Tbsp. minced onion
¼ cup flour
4 cups chicken broth
2 cups cooked wild rice
½ tsp. salt
1 cup half-and-half
2 Tbsp. dry sherry (optional)
Minced parsley or *chives*

1. Melt butter in saucepan and sauté onion until tender. Blend in flour, stirring constantly. Gradually add broth and cook, stirring constantly until mixture thickens slightly.
2. Stir in rice and salt and simmer about 5 minutes.
3. Blend in half-and-half and sherry and heat to serving temperature.
4. Garnish with minced parsley or chives and serve.

Makes 6 servings

DRY
SHER

Cream of Corn Crab Soup

Jul Hoober, New Holland, PA

8-oz. pkg. cream cheese
3 cups sour cream
2 7-oz. cans crab meat
Juice of ½ lemon
Salt and pepper to taste
¼ tsp. garlic powder
4 Tbsp. butter
4 Tbsp. flour
2-3 cups milk
1½-2 cups corn
1-2 cups croutons

1. Beat cream cheese until smooth. Add sour cream, crab, lemon juice and seasonings and mix well.
2. In a large saucepan melt butter. Add flour and cook until bubbly. Turn to low heat and slowly add milk, stirring constantly to make a smooth white sauce. Add corn and cream cheese mixture and heat through, stirring until smooth.
3. Serve with croutons.

Makes 10-12 servings

Seafood Soup

Irene Dewar, Pickering, ON

1 Tbsp. butter
2 Tbsp. green onions, minced
2 Tbsp. lemon juice
½ bay leaf
¼ tsp. dried thyme
2 cups whipping cream
1½ cups chicken stock
1 tsp. salt
1½ tsp. ground pepper
7-oz. can shrimp or *fish flakes*
1 tsp. cornstarch
1 Tbsp. water
2 Tbsp. sherry (optional)
1 Tbsp. parsley, chopped

1. Melt butter in large saucepan. Sauté onions. Add lemon juice, bay leaf and thyme and cook about 3-4 minutes until liquid is reduced, stirring frequently.
2. Blend in cream, chicken stock, salt, pepper and seafood. Slowly bring just to a boil. Reduce heat immediately.
3. Dissolve cornstarch in water and stir into soup. Simmer for 15 minutes.
4. Add sherry if desired and simmer an additional 5 minutes. Remove bay leaf. Ladle soup into heated bowls. Sprinkle with parsley and serve.

Makes 6 servings

Oyster Stew

Juanita Marner, Shipshewana, IN

8-oz. can oysters
2 Tbsp. margarine
1-1½ cups milk
¼ tsp. celery seed
Dash cayenne pepper
Dash paprika

1. Drain and reserve liquid from oysters.
2. Place margarine in 1-quart casserole dish. Microwave on high until melted, 30-45 seconds. Add oysters and cover. Microwave on high until edges are curled, 2-4 minutes.
3. Add enough milk to oyster liquid to measure 1½ cups. Add milk mixture, celery seed and cayenne pepper to oysters and cover. Microwave on medium high (70% power) until mixture is hot, 4 to 5 minutes. Sprinkle with paprika and serve.

Makes 2-4 servings

Chili California

Piecemakers Country Store, Costa Mesa, CA

1 cup chopped onion
½ cup chopped celery
1 cup diced jicama
½ cup sliced carrots
1 cup chopped green pepper
2 cloves garlic, minced
2 Tbsp. olive oil
2 beef bouillon cubes
1½ tsp. cumin
1½ tsp. chili powder
8-oz. can no-salt tomato sauce
2 16-oz. cans no-salt whole tomatoes, undrained
½ cup water
16-oz. can pinto beans, drained
16-oz. can chili beans, undrained
½ cup shredded cheddar cheese

1. In a Dutch oven sauté onion, celery, jicama, carrots, green pepper and garlic in oil until crisp tender. Add bouillon cubes, cumin, chili powder, tomato sauce, tomatoes and water. Bring to a boil.
2. Cover and simmer for 20 minutes, stirring occasionally. Uncover and simmer to desired thickness and until vegetables are tender, 10-20 minutes.
3. Stir in beans and heat through.
4. Sprinkle cheese over top and serve immediately.

Note: *This is a low-calorie chili which has lost none of its good full flavor.*

Makes 6-8 servings

Quilts and quiltings became a part of my life when I was very young. I have many fond memories of gathering with all the aunts and cousins at Grandma's house and playing around the quilt. Grandma made quilts for all of her children and some of her grandchildren. My mother made three quilts for each of her 15 children. I have continued the tradition, making quilts and comforters for my own children.

Mary Esther Yoder, Partridge, KS

Amish Chili

Catherine Esh, Spring Mills, PA

1 lb. lean ground beef
½ cup chopped onion
½ cup chopped celery
3 Tbsp. flour
¼ cup brown sugar
¼ cup ketchup
4 cups tomato juice
2-3 Tbsp. chili powder
16-oz. can kidney beans
Salt and pepper to taste

1. Brown ground beef, onion and celery. Drain excess fat. Add flour and heat through, stirring constantly. Add all remaining ingredients and mix well.
2. Cover and simmer 30 minutes. Serve.

Makes 6 servings

Ketchup
BUTTER
CHILI
POWDER

Crockpot Chili Con Carne

Katherine A. Schwartz, Freeport, IL

2 lbs. ground beef
2 cups chopped onion
2 cloves garlic, crushed
3 Tbsp. chili powder
1 tsp. salt
1 tsp. paprika
1 tsp. oregano
1 tsp. ground cumin
½ tsp. cayenne pepper
½ cup beef stock or *tomato juice*
28-oz. can tomatoes
16-oz. can red kidney beans
8-oz. pkg. macaroni

1. Brown beef in hot skillet. Drain excess fat.
2. Combine all ingredients except macaroni in crockpot, stirring well. Cook on low 8-10 hours or on high for 5 hours.
3. About 20 minutes before serving, prepare macaroni according to package directions.
4. Serve chili over macaroni.

Makes 8-10 servings

Taco Soup

Judy Miller, Hutchinson, KS
Marjorie Miller, Partridge, KS

1½ lbs. ground beef
½ cup chopped onion
28-oz. can whole tomatoes, undrained
16-oz. can kidney beans, undrained
17-oz. can corn, undrained
8-oz. can tomato sauce
1 pkg. dry taco seasoning
1-2 cups water
Salt and pepper to taste
1 cup shredded cheese
1 small bag nacho chips, crushed
1 cup sour cream

1. Brown beef in heavy kettle. Drain excess fat and add onion. Cook until onions are tender.
2. Add all remaining ingredients except cheese, nacho chips and sour cream. Simmer for 15 minutes.
3. Ladle into bowls and top with shredded cheese, nacho chips and sour cream. Serve.

Makes 6-8 servings

SOUR
CREAM

Cheeseburger Soup

Barbara Miller, Partridge, KS

1 lb. ground beef
3 cups chicken broth
½ cup grated carrots
¼ cup chopped onion
⅓ cup chopped celery
2 cups cooked rice
2 10¾-oz. cans cheddar cheese soup
2 soup cans milk
8-oz. carton sour cream
Salt and pepper to taste

1. Brown ground beef. Drain excess fat.
2. In large kettle combine broth, carrots, onion and celery. Bring to boil and simmer 10 minutes. Add ground beef, rice, soup and milk. Stir in sour cream and heat mixture through. Do not bring to a boil. (Thin with a little water if desired.)
3. Season to taste and serve.

Makes 6-8 servings

Summer Minestrone Soup

Dorothy Reise, Severna Park, MD

4 slices bacon, diced
1¼ Tbsp. olive oil
1 onion, chopped
1 clove garlic, crushed
2 carrots, chopped
2 stalks celery, chopped
5 cups water
5 beef bouillon cubes
1 large potato, diced
16-oz. can whole tomatoes
½ cup frozen peas
1½ Tbsp. tomato paste
½ cup uncooked macaroni
1½ Tbsp. chopped parsley
½ tsp. chopped oregano
Salt and pepper to taste
Grated Parmesan cheese

1. Sauté bacon briefly. Drain excess fat.
2. Heat oil in a large saucepan. Add onion, garlic, carrots, celery and bacon. Cook until onion is soft and transparent.
3. Dissolve bouillon cubes in water to make a stock.
4. Add stock, remaining vegetables and tomato paste to saucepan. Cover and cook over low heat for about 40 minutes.
5. Add macaroni, parsley and oregano and cook about 15-20 minutes longer. Add salt and pepper to taste. Serve with grated Parmesan cheese.

Note: *Add sliced zucchini or string beans to vegetables when in season.*

Makes 6 servings

Crazy quilts have always reminded me of minestrone. You add bits and pieces of wonderful vegetables to the soup, providing a rich color and texture. For a beautiful crazy quilt you need bits and pieces of wonderful fabric to achieve a richness in color and texture.

Frances D. Bents, Annapolis, MD

MINESTRONE

Pat Garrow, Lodi, CA

2 garlic cloves, crushed
4 green onions, finely chopped
2 Tbsp. chopped fresh parsley
2 carrots, sliced
1 large onion, chopped
4 celery stalks, diced
¼ cup olive oil
28-oz. can whole tomatoes, undrained
2 quarts water
16-oz. can refried beans
1 cup uncooked pasta
Salt and pepper to taste

1. In large saucepan sauté garlic, onions, parsley, carrots, onion and celery in olive oil.
2. Chop tomatoes. Add chopped tomatoes with juice, water and beans to saucepan with vegetables and cook on low for 2 hours, stirring frequently.
3. Stir in pasta and cook 1 more hour, stirring occasionally. Season to taste and serve.

Makes 8-10 servings

Herbed Cheese Topping for Minestrone

Frances D. Bents, Annapolis, MD

1 cup Parmesan cheese
4 Tbsp. butter, softened
¼ cup finely ground walnuts
1 clove garlic, minced
1½ Tbsp. minced parsley
½ tsp. chervil
½ tsp. basil
½ tsp. marjoram

1. Combine all ingredients in blender or small bowl and blend or mix until just smooth.
2. Serve minestrone in individual bowls. Top each serving with herbed cheese topping.

Makes 6 servings

I was introduced to quilting by my grandparents. Grandmother did custom quilting for people in the Chicago area in the 1940s. Grandfather always traced the quilting patterns for her. I think they must have spent many evenings together tracing and quilting.

Susan G. Sneer, Mountain Lake, MN

CHEDDAR CHOWDER

Lena Hoover, Narvon, PA
Emma Martin, Lititz, PA

2 cups water
2 cups diced potatoes
½ cup diced carrots
½ cup diced celery
¼ cup chopped onion
1 tsp. salt
¼ tsp. pepper
4 Tbsp. butter
½ cup flour
2 cups milk
¼ cup grated cheddar cheese
1 cup cubed ham or *hot dogs*

1. Combine water, potatoes, carrots, celery, onion, salt and pepper in large kettle and cook 10-12 minutes.
2. Meanwhile, prepare a white sauce in small saucepan by melting butter. Stir in flour until smooth. Slowly add milk and cook until thickened. Stir in cheese until melted.
3. Drain vegetables thoroughly and stir in cheese sauce. Add ham or hot dogs and heat until almost boiling point. Serve.

Makes 6 servings

CREAM

Cheese Soup

Katy J. Widger, Los Lunas, NM

2 Tbsp. butter or *margarine*
¾ cup finely chopped onion
1 clove garlic, minced
½ lb. cheddar cheese, grated
½ lb. Swiss or *Stilton cheese, grated*
⅓ cup flour
3 cups chicken broth
1 cup half-and-half
⅓ cup dry white wine (optional)
Salt and pepper to taste
1 bay leaf

1. Melt butter in large, heavy saucepan. Sauté onion and garlic until onion is wilted.
2. On a piece of waxed paper sprinkle grated cheeses and flour. Add to saucepan, stirring to mix cheeses, flour, onion and garlic thoroughly and quickly. Remove from heat.
3. Gradually add chicken broth, half-and-half and wine if desired. Bring to a boil slowly over medium heat. Add salt, pepper and bay leaf. Simmer for 10 minutes. Remove bay leaf and serve.

Makes 8 servings

Baked Onion Soup

Jean Harris Robinson, Cinnaminson, NJ

Beef Broth

4 small beef and 2 small veal bones
2 carrots, chopped
4 sprigs parsley
1 Tbsp. salt (optional)
8 peppercorns
2 quarts water

Soup

Beef broth
5 beef bouillon cubes
Water
4 large onions, very thinly sliced
½ lb. butter
1 loaf French bread, very thinly sliced
1 lb. Swiss cheese, very thinly sliced
15-20 sprigs parsley

1. To prepare broth combine all ingredients in a large pot and bring to a boil. Skim, then simmer for approximately 3 hours. Strain through a sieve. Cool broth and store in refrigerator overnight. Discard layer of hardened fat that will form on top of broth.
2. To prepare soup reheat broth to warm. Stir in bouillon cubes which have been dissolved in a little warm water. Add enough water to make two quarts broth.
3. In separate pan sauté onions in butter until soft and golden. Set aside.

4. In three 2-quart casserole dishes arrange the following as if you were preparing lasagna: 1 cup broth, layer of onions, layer of bread and layer of cheese. Repeat layers until casserole dishes are full, ending with layers of cheese.
5. Divide remaining broth over the three casseroles. Store in refrigerator until ready to bake.
6. Bake at 350 F. for 1 hour.
7. This soup will be thick. Spoon into small shallow bowls or mugs. Add sprig of parsley for garnish.

Note: *This recipe may be made with 4-5 cans beef or chicken broth, but the extra flavor in the homemade broth is well worth the effort.*

Makes 10-12 servings

When my mother-in-law gave me a pieced quilt top, I decided not to just put it away in a closet. Instead I borrowed a quilting frame and with the help of two women in my church taught myself to quilt. I was hooked and have been quilting ever since.

Janet Yocum, Elizabethtown, PA

Easy French Onion Soup

Mary Puskar, Baltimore, MD

4 cups sliced onions
¼ cup margarine
¼ cup flour
6 cups water
¼ cup beef bouillon granules
6 slices French bread, cubed
1 cup grated mozzarella cheese

1. In a large saucepan sauté onions in margarine. Cook over low heat until onions are tender, stirring occasionally. Sprinkle with flour and cook for 2 minutes, stirring constantly.
2. Add water and beef bouillon. Heat until boiling, cover and simmer another 20 minutes.
3. Ladle soup into oven-proof bowls and top with French bread. Top with grated cheese and place under broiler until cheese melts and is bubbly. Serve immediately.

Makes 6-8 servings

Creamy Tomato Soup

Flossie Sultzaberger, Mechanicsburg, PA

2 Tbsp. finely chopped onion
1 Tbsp. butter or *margarine*
1½ lbs. ripe tomatoes
¼ cup water
1 Tbsp. minced fresh basil
1 Tbsp. sugar
2 Tbsp. butter
2 Tbsp. all-purpose flour
½ tsp. salt
¼ tsp. white pepper
2 cups milk

1. In microwave-safe bowl combine onion with 1 Tbsp. butter. Microwave on high 2 minutes or until onion has softened.
2. Peel, seed and chop tomatoes. Reserve ¼ cup for garnish. Add remaining tomatoes to onion mixture with water, basil and sugar. Stir and microwave on high 4½-5 minutes until tomatoes are softened, stirring once more.
3. In 2-quart bowl microwave 2 Tbsp. butter on high 30 seconds. Whisk in flour, salt and pepper. Stir in milk. Microwave on high 4-5 minutes or until thickened, stirring frequently.
4. In food processor or blender process tomato mixture slowly, pouring in milk mixture.
5. Garnish with reserved chopped tomato and serve hot or chilled.

Makes 4 servings

My friend and I planned a bridal shower for a mutual friend. Tired of the usual boring games, I invited each person who attended the shower to design one block for a sampler wall hanging. It was great fun watching persons who thought they had no talent use my supplies and suggestions to piece together wonderful designs. I had a hard time parting with the finished wall hanging!

Rebecca Eldredge, Honolulu, HI

DILL
WEED

Tomato Soup

Helen Gerber, Stoughton, WI

28-oz. can tomatoes, undrained
1 small onion, sliced
2 stalks celery, chopped
6 Tbsp. butter or *margarine*
6 Tbsp. flour
4 cups milk
½ Tbsp. dill weed
Pepper to taste
¾ cup shredded cheddar cheese

1. Cut tomatoes into bite-sized pieces. In saucepan bring tomatoes, onion and celery to a boil. Boil for 5 minutes.
2. In large soup kettle melt butter. Blend in flour and cook until smooth and bubbly. Gradually add milk, stirring constantly.
3. Slowly add hot tomato mixture to white sauce, stirring constantly. Season with dill weed and pepper.
4. Immediately before serving, top with cheddar cheese.

Makes 8 servings

Puréed Carrot Soup

Kathy Hardis Fraeman, Olney, MD

1½ Tbsp. cooking oil
1-2 cups coarsely chopped leeks
1 clove garlic, minced
4 cups coarsely chopped carrots
1 large potato, coarsely chopped
4-6 cups water or *chicken stock*
½ tsp. salt
Pepper to taste
1 cup croutons

1. In a large soup kettle heat oil. Sauté leeks and garlic until softened, but not browned.
2. Add carrots, potato and enough liquid to barely cover. Simmer about 30 minutes until vegetables are softened.
3. Purée soup in blender. Return to soup pot and add remaining liquid to desired consistency. Stir in salt and pepper, mix well and heat through. Mix well and heat through.
4. Serve hot or cold with croutons.

Makes 4-6 servings

Split Pea Soup

Barbara Forrester Landis, Lititz, PA

1 lb. dry green split peas
1 ham hock
1 cup chopped onion
1 tsp. chicken bouillon granules
8 cups water
½ tsp. salt
¼ tsp. pepper
1 cup sliced carrots
1 cup chopped celery
½ cup milk or *light cream*
2 Tbsp. butter or *margarine*

1. In a kettle combine peas, ham hock, onion, bouillon granules, water, salt and pepper. Bring to a boil. Cover and simmer 1½ hours, stirring frequently.
2. Remove ham bone, debone and return meat to soup. Add carrots and celery and simmer another 30 minutes.
3. Stir milk and butter into soup and heat through. Serve.

Makes 8 servings

Pumpkin Soup

Winnie Friese, Washington, NJ

1 quart chicken stock
29-oz. can pumpkin
12-oz. can evaporated milk
¼ cup whole milk
1 cup chopped onion
8 Tbsp. margarine
1 Tbsp. flour
¼ tsp. nutmeg
¼ tsp. ginger

1. In a large saucepan heat chicken stock. Add pumpkin, evaporated milk and whole milk and continue heating.
2. Sauté onion in margarine. Add flour, nutmeg and ginger and cook until bubbly. Stir into soup and heat mixture until piping hot. Do NOT boil. Serve.

Makes 6 servings

PUMPKIN

Gazpacho

Ann Foss, Brooklyn, NY

4 cups tomato juice
2 beef bouillon cubes
2 large tomatoes
½ cup chopped cucumbers
¼ cup chopped green pepper
¼ cup chopped onion
¼ cup wine vinegar
2 Tbsp. cooking oil
½ tsp. salt
1 tsp. Worcestershire sauce
6 drops Tabasco

1. Bring tomato juice to a boil in large saucepan. Add beef bouillon cubes and stir to dissolve. Remove from heat and cool.
2. Peel, seed and dice tomatoes. Dice, but do not peel, cucumbers.
3. Add tomatoes, cucumbers and all remaining ingredients to cooled broth and mix well.
4. Refrigerate and serve in chilled bowls or mugs.

Makes 8 servings

Zucchini Soup

Janet S. Gillespie, Gilbertsville, KY

2 tsp. cooking oil
1 cup chopped onion
1 clove garlic, minced
4 medium zucchini, coarsely chopped
4 tsp. chicken-flavored bouillon granules
1 Tbsp. lemon juice
3 cups water
2 tsp. dill
½ cup sour cream

1. In large saucepan heat oil over medium-low heat. Sauté onion and garlic about 5 minutes or until soft.
2. Stir in zucchini, chicken bouillon granules, lemon juice and water and bring to a boil. Reduce heat and simmer 15 minutes.
3. Purée mixture in food processor or blender. Pour into serving dish and quickly whisk in dill and sour cream. Serve.

Makes 4 servings

Cheese Broccoli Soup

Lola Kennel, Strang, NE

1 small onion, chopped
2 Tbsp. butter
3 Tbsp. flour
2 cups milk
2 chicken bouillon cubes
1½ cups boiling water
2 cups shredded cheese
½ tsp. salt
½ tsp. thyme
1 Tbsp. garlic salt
Dash pepper
1 cup cooked, chopped broccoli

1. Sauté onion in butter until tender. Stir in flour and heat until bubbly. Gradually add milk and heat slowly, stirring constantly.
2. Dissolve bouillon cubes in boiling water. Add to white sauce with cheese, salt, thyme, garlic salt and pepper and heat through.
3. Stir in cooked broccoli and serve.

Makes 4-6 servings

Country Cabbage Soup

Bea Marxen, Bellville, TX

½ lb. ground beef
4 cups shredded green cabbage
1 cup finely diced potatoes
1 cup finely diced carrots
½ cup chopped onion
3 Tbsp. butter
1 Tbsp. flour
1½ cups beef broth
1½ cups ranch dressing

1. Brown beef in large saucepan and drain excess fat.
2. Add cabbage, potatoes, carrots and onion. Stir in butter and cook until potatoes are tender but not brown, about 5 minutes. Stir in flour.
3. Add remaining ingredients and simmer about 20 minutes. Serve.

Makes 4-6 servings

My husband frequently brings fabric home from his business trips. One year I decided to make a Double Wedding Ring wall hanging with the pieces. For us, each piece of fabric in the finished product has a story of its own.

Alana Robbins, Los Lunas, NM

Bean and Potato Soup

Jan Carroll, Morton, IL

3 lbs. mixed beans
16-oz. can chicken broth
3-5 stalks celery, diced
1 onion, chopped
1 carrot, grated
1 bay leaf
5-7 new potatoes, diced
4 cups water
8-oz. can tomato sauce

1. Prepare beans according to directions, soaking if needed.
2. Combine all ingredients except tomato sauce in a Dutch oven or large soup kettle. Simmer 2-6 hours. After 2 hours add tomato sauce and heat through. Remove bay leaf before serving.
3. If desired, add more water during last half hour to dilute soup to desired consistency.

Makes 6 servings

Beef Chili with Zucchini

Sue Gierhart, Voorhees, NJ

¾ lb. lean ground meat
1½ cups chopped onions
1½ lbs. zucchini
16-oz. can red kidney beans
28-oz. can tomatoes
6-oz. can tomato paste
½ cup water
1 Tbsp. chili powder
1 tsp. cumin
4 cups cooked brown rice
¾ cup shredded sharp cheddar cheese
6 green onions, minced

1. Cook ground meat and onions in 4-quart Dutch oven over medium-high heat, stirring frequently.
2. Cut zucchini into small pieces. Drain and rinse kidney beans.
3. When meat is browned, add zucchini, beans, tomatoes, tomato paste, water, chili powder and cumin. Stir gently just until blended. Cover and simmer for 10 minutes. Uncover and simmer 15 minutes longer, stirring occasionally.
4. Spoon over rice. Sprinkle with cheese and green onions. Serve.

Makes 6 servings

KIDNEY
CUMIN

Ham Chowder

Betty Sereno, Terra Alta, WV

2 cups diced potatoes
1 cup green beans
1 carrot, diced
2 cups water
1½ tsp. salt or *less*
4 Tbsp. margarine
2 cups diced ham
1 cup chopped onion
2 10¾-oz. cans cream of mushroom soup
3 cups milk
Pepper to taste

1. In a saucepan combine potatoes, green beans, carrot, water and salt. Cook until potatoes and carrot are tender.
2. Heat margarine in skillet and sauté ham and onion. Add to potato mixture.
3. Add cream of mushroom soup and milk. Blend and heat through. Season to taste and serve.

Makes 6 servings

CHICKEN SOUP

Elaine Untracht Pawelko, Monroe Township, NJ

5-lb. stewing hen
Water to cover
1 tsp. salt or *less*
1 large onion, diced
3 ribs celery, chopped
2 carrots, diced
1 small parsnip, diced
2 small turnips, sliced
1-2 leeks, diced
1 small handful fresh dill sprigs

1. Rinse chicken and trim off excess fat. Place in soup pot. Add giblets from hen. Add water to cover and salt. Cover pot and heat to boiling. Uncover and skim.
2. Add vegetables to pot. Cover and simmer over low heat for 2 hours. Remove chicken from soup. Debone and cut meat into bite-sized pieces. Return chicken to broth.
3. Add dill sprigs and heat through.

Note: *Soup is best when made a day in advance. Before reheating, remove excess fat which has formed on top.*

Makes 8 servings

Cheesy Turkey Chowder

Mrs. Mahlon Miller, Hutchinson, KS

2 turkey wings or *1 turkey drumstick*
1 tsp. salt
1 medium onion, chopped
1 cup chopped carrots
1 cup chopped celery
1 cup chopped potatoes
2 cups milk
6 Tbsp. flour
4 Tbsp. butter
1 cup shredded cheddar cheese

1. In a large saucepan cook turkey, salt and onion in water to cover. Simmer until meat is tender.
2. Remove meat from broth. Cool, debone and dice into small pieces. Set aside.
3. Add water to make 4 cups broth. Add carrots, celery and potatoes and simmer until tender.
4. Gradually blend milk into flour until mixture is smooth. Stir milk and flour mixture into turkey broth. Add butter and cheese and cook over medium heat until thickened, stirring constantly.
5. Add turkey meat to chowder and heat through. Serve.

Makes 6 servings

Mom's Vegetable Beef Soup

Janis Landefeld, Baltimore, MD

1¼ lbs. ground beef
3 ribs celery, sliced
3 carrots, sliced
1 medium onion, chopped
5 beef bouillon cubes
5 cups boiling water
16-oz. can tomatoes, undrained
1 tsp. dried basil
Salt and pepper to taste
1 Tbsp. Kitchen Bouquet
2 cups frozen vegetables
3-4 cups cooked barley or *cooked pasta*

1. Combine ground beef, celery, carrots and onion in large soup pot. Cook over medium high heat until ground beef is completely browned. Drain excess fat.
2. Dissolve bouillon cubes in boiling water.
3. Add bouillon, tomatoes, basil, salt, pepper, Kitchen Bouquet and vegetables to soup pot. Simmer about 20 minutes.
4. Immediately before serving, stir in cooked pasta or barley. Serve with a loaf of homemade bread.
5. For thinner soup add more bouillon broth.

Makes 8 large servings

Hamburger Vegetable Soup

Ruth Ann Penner, Hillsboro, KS

1¼ lbs. ground beef
1½ quarts water
½ cup chopped celery
2 cups diced potatoes
1 large onion, chopped
1 cup chopped carrots
Salt and pepper to taste
10¾-oz. can tomato soup
½ cup minute rice

1. Bring raw hamburger to a good boil in 1½ quarts water. Add celery, potatoes, onion, carrots, salt and pepper. Simmer 45-60 minutes.
2. Add tomato soup and rice and simmer another 2-3 minutes. Serve.

Variation: *Substitute 46-oz. can V-8 juice for water. Omit potatoes. Substitute 10¾-oz. can cream of celery soup for tomato soup. Add dash of sugar and basil. Follow other directions and heat through.*

Judi Robb, Manhattan, KS

Makes 6 servings

Potato Soup

Silva Beachy, Millersburg, OH

6-8 slices bacon
4 large potatoes, diced
¼ tsp. salt (optional)
1 onion, chopped
2 carrots, diced
½ cup butter
¾ cup flour
4 cups milk
½ cup grated cheese

1. Fry bacon until crisp. Crumble and set aside.
2. To bacon drippings add potatoes, onion, carrots and salt if desired. Add enough water to cover vegetables. Boil until potatoes are tender.
3. Meanwhile, melt butter in separate saucepan. Add flour and stir until smooth, cooking about 1 minute. Add milk, blending until smooth, and cook until mixture thickens, stirring constantly.
4. Add white sauce to cooked vegetables and heat through. (For a thinner soup add more milk.)
5. Immediately before serving, add reserved bacon. Garnish with grated cheese.

Makes 6-8 servings

Potato Rivel Soup

Linda Baker, Arnold, MD

Soup

8 Tbsp. butter
1 small onion, diced
1½ quarts water
2 medium potatoes, cubed
2 stalks celery, diced
1 large onion, diced
1 tsp. celery seed
Salt and pepper to taste

Rivels

1 cup minus 2 Tbsp. flour
Dash salt and pepper
1 egg

1. Melt butter in 3-quart pan until browned. Add small onion and brown until very dark. Discard onion. Add water and bring to a boil. Add vegetables and celery seed and bring to a boil.
2. To prepare rivels put flour in a bowl. Stir in salt and pepper. Make a well and drop egg into well. Stir with a fork until crumbly.
3. Drop rivels, one tablespoon at a time, into boiling soup. Simmer for 20-30 minutes.
4. Season with salt and pepper and serve.

Makes 4 servings

Hot and Sour Soup

Marlene Fonken, Upland, CA

10 ozs. boneless, skinless chicken breast
6½ cups chicken broth
2 cups shredded Chinese cabbage
2 cups shredded carrots
2 cups sliced fresh mushrooms
1 Tbsp. soy sauce
12 ozs. tofu
¼ cup rice vinegar
½ tsp. pepper
¼ cup cornstarch
¼ cup water
4-5 green onion tops, diced

1. Cut uncooked chicken breast into strips.
2. Combine chicken breast, chicken broth, cabbage, carrots, mushrooms and soy sauce and bring to a boil. Reduce heat and simmer for 5 minutes.
3. Cut tofu into strips.
4. Add tofu, rice vinegar and pepper to chicken soup and bring to a boil again. Boil for 1 minute.
5. Combine cornstarch and water and stir into soup. Heat, stirring until slightly thickened.
6. Immediately before serving, sprinkle with green onion tops.

Makes 12 servings

Creamy Vegetable Soup

Christine H. Weaver, Reinholds, PA

1 Tbsp. margarine
3 medium carrots, thinly sliced
1 medium pepper, chopped
1 medium onion, chopped
16-oz. can whole tomatoes, chopped
3-4 potatoes
2 cups water
1 tsp. chicken bouillon
1½ cups skim milk
1 Tbsp. prepared mustard

1. In heavy frying pan over medium heat melt margarine. Add very thin carrots and peppers and sauté until lightly browned. Add onions and sauté until vegetables have softened.
2. Drain juice from tomatoes and add chopped tomatoes to vegetables. Continue cooking over medium heat.
3. Meanwhile, in soup kettle dissolve chicken bouillon in water. Cook potatoes in chicken broth until softened. Pour into food processor and blend until smooth.
4. Return to kettle and add milk, mustard and vegetables. Heat over low heat. Do not bring to a boil. Serve when heated through.

Makes 4-6 servings

Sweet and Sour Cabbage Soup

Freda Gail Stern, Dallas, TX

3-4-lb. chuck roast with bone
9 cups water
2-lb. head cabbage, shredded
1½ cups diced onion
3-4 carrots, sliced
2 stalks celery, diced
2 16-oz. cans tomatoes
8 gingersnaps
1 tsp. salt
½ tsp. celery salt
½ tsp. dill weed
Freshly ground pepper to taste
⅓ cup white sugar
¼ cup light brown sugar
1 tsp. sour salt (citric acid)

INDEX

1. In large soup kettle combine chuck roast and water and bring to a boil. Simmer for ½ hour. Skim water.
2. Add cabbage, onion, carrots, celery, tomatoes, gingersnaps and all seasonings except sugars and sour salt. Bring to a boil. Lower heat and simmer 3-4 hours.
3. Add sugars and sour salt. Cook over medium heat for 15 minutes. Taste and adjust seasoning as desired.
4. Cool and refrigerate for at least one day before serving.
5. Before reheating remove bone, cutting meat into bite-sized pieces. Reheat and serve.

Makes 10 servings

When I think of quilting today, I always return to my earliest memories of hiding underneath my grandmother's quilting frame in a small clapboard house in the wooded hills of Kentucky. The frame was built from spare planks nailed at the corners and hung from the ceiling by ropes. Several times a week my mother, grandmother and her friends would gather in her front room for a "bee." I would sit underneath at my mother's feet, watching the needles dart in and out of the muslin with rhythmic precision. It was always the quilters' hands that most fascinated me. How did they manage to hold the needle so delicately and guide it with such purpose? My favorite part of those quilting days was poking my hand into the quilt from underneath amid the stern warnings of my mother and the giggles of my friends.

Laura Barrus Bishop, Boerne, TX